An Angel Visits Mary

Original Spanish version by Mada Carreño
Illustrator: Bety Fischman

Bible Stories for Children

NOVALIS

Like all the other young people in Nazareth, Mary always got up early in the morning. After washing with cold water out in the yard, she would help her mother with the household chores. She kneaded flour to make bread and went to the well for water.

Everybody was talking about the fact that she would soon be marrying a carpenter who lived in the town. He was called Joseph.

One afternoon when Mary was alone in the house, a young person with a heavenly smile appeared before her. All around him was a strange brightness. He raised his hand and said,

"Hail, Mary. You are full of grace and the Lord is with you."

Mary was frightened by what she saw. She didn't understand what she was hearing.

"Don't be scared," he said to her. "God has sent me to tell you that you are going to have a baby and that you are to call him Jesus."

"How can this be?" Mary asked; "I'm not even married yet."

"Everything is possible with God," said the angel. "You should know that your cousin Elizabeth is going to have a baby, too, even though she is quite old. Her baby will be called John. Your child will be called the Son of God."

"I will do whatever God wants me to do," said Mary.

Some time later she married Joseph. They were waiting for the child to be born, when the government said they had to go to the village of Bethlehem to put their names on the official list. The trip took several days. Joseph led the donkey that carried Mary and their supplies for the journey.

When they got to Bethlehem it was already getting dark and all the hotels were full. Joseph knocked on the doors of several houses to see if he could rent a room, but he had no luck. Finally, one of the villagers said that Joseph and Mary could stay in a nearby cave that he used as a stable for his animals.

Joseph found some branches to sweep the stable floor. Then he took armfuls of clean hay to make a bed for Mary. She lay down and Joseph covered her with his woollen cloak.

Then he settled the donkey beside an ox.

Not long after, the child was born. Mary wrapped him in swaddling clothes and placed him in a manger filled with straw to keep him warm.

In the fields around Bethlehem shepherds were guarding their sheep. Suddenly they saw many heavenly beings in the sky, and an angel appeared to the shepherds. They were very frightened.

"Don't be afraid," said the angel. I have come to tell you that the baby just born in Bethlehem is the Christ, the Son of God. You will find him in a cave, sleeping in a manger."

The shepherds hurried to see the child. They took some small gifts with them. And all the while many angels were singing in the heavens,

"Glory to God in the highest,
and peace to God's people on earth."